I can only hope after you are done reading this, you will feel a love for her. The kind of love that walks inside of me every day.

Karnes

Captions of My Soul
Vol. 1

Original Prose

KARNES

Dear, Courage

I want to have the courage to tell you how I feel one day. You'd think telling someone you care about how you feel would be easy, but it's always been intimidating for me when my feelings are as strong for you as they are now. I don't necessarily fear rejection. I fear the process of expressing what took months to say, only for it to be appreciated, but not reciprocated. I understand that's life. Some of us get the answer we want, while the rest of us spill our guts only to have them be left there. We walk around empty on the inside for years to come without a sense of direction, because once you lose your way, circles seem to feel better on the bones. I imagine you sitting in front of me, talking about everything on your mind and me nodding at you with adoration, because you know I hear you. I've come across many who would forgo an entire life of love and adventure for the safety they feel being close to someone who is just there in physical form, without a passion that could hang the moon permanently in the sky. To watch you breathe would be the most beautiful lifetime for me. Events like that haven't happened to me as of late. When I say as of late, I mean years. I lie to myself to make the ache less of a feeling and more of a happenstance. I see her every night in some form, but dreams are where I hear her voice. It's where I see what we could've become. I don't know how to get to you without shedding my flesh for the reasons why love may be different this time. I say love, because after you care for someone long enough, it becomes paramount to give it its proper name. You said you were waiting anxiously to read these words. That you were waiting to read what I came up with. I hope knowing how I feel can make you see where I'm standing when I feel far away from you. I hope you feel my hands in yours when the lights go out and your breath exceeds a calming sensation. I'll always wonder about you and how you are, because I truly do care for your well-being. I hate how much distance resides between our talks. I hate how much you don't know about me. You've held my head and my heart. Give me your breath always. I couldn't take another one without yours.

A Million Moons

Growing up is nothing more than enduring growing pains. I want nothing more than to grow with you. You dropped your soul on the bedroom floor long before I ever stepped into your life. It's what keeps me here. I don't know where your love comes from. I simply want to hold you all day and watch the world with you. Love is a full moon. It's a shared breath. It's honest. It's inviting. It's you. It's always present in the energy exchanges you give to me. I know we don't fully know each other, but the mere possibility of it being you down the road has me aching for an adventure I've always wanted to take. It's insane how much I miss you. It's an incredible amount for never actually holding you. I miss you as if I've loved you before. As if I've shared a million moons with you. I'm trying to put everything into perspective and understand how you've embedded yourself not only in my life and dreams, but in my goddamn soul. I'm lucky to have you like this. To get to know you. To get to write about you. To fucking know you at all. I don't take any of it lightly. Knowing your breath to be the words, wraps me in comfort. It's always been you. You're it for me. However intense or over the top it sounds, I'm on this earth to find a way to get closer to you. I fucking miss you. I just want to love you before my breath turns into empty air that still holds your name. Use my soul as your bed. Use my hands to paint what your eyes see. I may hold back some, because there is only so much we can do about our current situation. I'll always do my best to live in this moment without getting ahead of myself, even if my writings speak differently. I know there will be a day when everything aligns to the sun in me and the moon in you. I love that you enjoy being here and choose to be here. It's the first time someone has chosen to do that. You've changed my love for myself. When you find someone who puts reason behind your past, you do everything you can to make them your future. I'll always adore your ability to translate the words that escape me when it comes to defining who you are. I can see the rest of my life when I catch the light coming from your eyes.

Be Bold, Sweet One

It is a place where few often go. A place locked away in the hiding hills that wrap around spiraling waterfalls. Trees that whisper all the things strangers talk about. The secrets do not just hide. They hide in plain sight. Loneliness kills off the doubt growing in the tall grass beside the lily pads. A symphony erupts from the animals waking up to see the red sun and clear skies. There you can see a dream being born. It rises from the dense and heavy fog tumbling through the valleys. It gets quiet. Pitch perfect silence. Then, a howl sets off every fiber in your being. It awakens the dead and makes you take notice of your surroundings. You are a dream. Every single one of them. Sometimes, dreams notice each other, and other times they go unappreciated. Even if you must go alone, be bold in your adventure. A dream is nothing without the constant pursuit of the soul.

Questions to Ponder

The night will always be where my secrets make love to any truth they can find. From the time I could remember, all I knew was you. The universe created souls in order for humans to find love. What we have is something death will never be able to steal or borrow. Stay with me and I will stay with you. May the moon and sun keep bringing us a light to share for the rest of our days. We will continue being a pair of hearts, looking for the next adventure to take. Life is better when you leave behind everything that never needed to be a part of your journey. Where did you come from and how did you stay so unbelievably beautiful? All I know, is what we have and what we will be, happened because we already were.

Lost, but proud to be

I've had more than enough chances. After everything I have been through, I know this time is where things come together. We do not always get what we want, but we do always get what we deserve. Focus on what is important in your life and go from there. I made a road trip recently, which turned out to be a life journey and something I needed to do. I am more than what others have told me I wasn't. I am not perfect, but I do try to be honest and fair. Making necessary steps to get back on track and finally starting a life that I will be able to share with someone. If you think you are lost, do not worry. We all are. Some of us just make it look like we know what we are doing.

Looking in, only to look out

I saw this woman today who was walking the streets of San Antonio with six random bags belonging to her. I wondered to myself if she carries them all the time or if it was a shopping spree. She was dressed as if life had not gone her way, while being mismatched head to toe. Her hair was up in a bun. Her shoes had seen many of roads and dirt trails. Countless stories are held within each breath of wind that passes through her. Her face looked anxious, as if she didn't know where to go to next, but you could tell she was strong in force, in herself. It takes moxie for someone to walk the streets without worrying about what others think. Especially those who wonder if she has ever had a chance to go on a shopping spree. She walked past the restaurant's outstretched arms and out of my sight. Her mind is wondering if the windows looking in, think about the same things when they are looking out.

Loving with all we have

There are things we can write about and then there are things we need to be a part of. I am thankful to be alongside you on this journey. You have filled many of notebooks, just you did with the spaces in my heart. You make me a better me. Someone like you is something you don't find in a lifetime. I was at the beach for two hours today and my only wish was me wanting you with me. To know that I can think about you whenever I want and call, message, and reach out to you at any time, gives me immense joy and love. You are my ocean. You are each wave that makes up my shoreline. I closed my eyes and saw us dancing in the water like we will one day. We are happy together. We are in love with each other. That's all we need to make our love outlast everything else we don't have control over.

JUMP

I've been living life afraid and with uncertainty. I was raised to always believe in myself, no matter the situation I was faced with. At times it is hard to live up to that standard. At times it's easier doing the minimum required. Playing it safe and not exploring. Waiting for something to happen, instead of making shit happen for yourself. I took this road trip with a few things in mine and so far, I have overcome a lot of my self-doubt and anxiety about being on my own. I am a human. Most of what is going on in my head is self-induced. I am relearning who I am. I am relearning what I want. I am balancing life, work, and priorities now. It feels good being on top of your own mountain after settling for trails that kept you safe. Explore. Reach new goals. Failing is only possible if you're trying. Success comes shortly after. I am looking forward to seeing what the rest of the trip has in store for me. I got the word, "jump," tattooed on the fingers of my right hand. It is my reminder to go after what I want. To never settle for the scraps I find. To make something of my life and not wait on my chance. It is there to give me meaning that every chance not taken, is an opportunity I will never get again.

Behind the Blinds

I often give myself to too many things at once. I believe others have the same intentions as I do, when that is hardly the case. I think it will be different. I think I will help and allow others to see a different able of the universe they haven't seen before. I help too much, but I don't know how not to. I remember being twelve years old and my mother was out in the garage around 12am, smoking and drinking a beer. The blinds on the door were shut, but I couldn't help but to open them just enough with my fingers to see what was going on and why my mother was up at that hour. I saw her crying. They weren't silent ones you hide and keep to yourself. They were a plea for help, but it was only me up at the time. It completely broke me. Regardless of what she had done to my brothers and I at the time, she was still my mother. I opened the door and went outside to sit next to her. I held her. I listened to her. I just wanted her to know I was there. That is all we need at times. Having someone there. It happened on several occasions during that time in my life. She went through a lot, hell, we all did after the divorce. I talk to her today as if we had always been close, but that wasn't always the case. I've learned forgiveness in my later years. I was born a helper, a peacemaker, a giver of time, a healer of sorts, and how to be vulnerable. I don't blame anyone for leaving. I left many times myself. Even though I give a lot of my time away, I wouldn't change it for putting me where I am now in my own life. Leaving oftentimes leads us to a new beginning, and I can only hope others find it to be as welcoming as mine has been for me and to me.

I'm tired of dying; my grave is full.

I've been alive for nine years. I've died before and my mind was the murderer. For too long, I allowed it to ruin who I was and take advantage of my personal journey. I had a failed suicide attempt in May of 2009. I have my scars to look at each day to know I am alive for a reason. I took any pill I could find. I drank an entire bottle of Jose Cuervo. I ran the water in the tub and got in. The rest I will save due to the graphic nature of it. My grave has many versions of who I was and who I have been. I grew tired of living scared and full of anxiety. October 23rd will be 6th year of sobriety. My life changed that night when I made the choice to leave alcohol behind for good and begin focusing on my life. It hasn't been easy, and I still have my bad days, but I don't have a bad life. I know the hell I have been through. I am a better man, human, son, brother, and friend, because I knew if I didn't get sober, I wouldn't make it much longer. To all of those who are struggling, you aren't alone. You never will be. Reach out to me if you feel compelled to do so. Even if you don't, I plead to you that you find someone to talk about it with. I love you. If you are hurting, I am sorry. It gets better though. If my life can, yours can. I promise you.

H(old) O(n) P(ain) E(nds)

"I walked back to pick up the dreams and stars I had lost in the nightmare I survived."

It took a few months for my arms to heal after doing what I did to them. I can still hear the cutting sounds and feel the sensations from that night, in my mind, there was no other alternative. My mind was made up during the walk back the morning after I left the holding cell. It was my 2nd DUI in three months. My PTSD, anxiety, and depression were in full force. I just couldn't see a way out of the hell I had put myself in. I was tired of hurting and being in pain. I was trying to kill whatever was inside of me. I was tired of drinking to escape life. I was as spent as a human could possibly be. Before being released from the hospital, the doctor told me that I came within 3mm of dying. It sticks with me to this day. The smallest of margins between life and death, became the distance that saved my life in the end. I called my mom first. I was basically ordered to do so. It was the last thing on my mind at the time. She cried, and said, "I am so sorry I couldn't save you or help you." She was so distraught that her middle child almost killed himself. I knew it would take her a while to be okay, if ever. I called my dad next. He cried and said the same thing. They both reiterated how much they loved me. I don't know what else could have been said. I already felt their emotions which were enough for me to know how devastating it all turned out to be. You don't have to die to kill yourself. I hung up the phone and stared out of the hospital window. The sky never felt so close in my life. They were both as shocked as everyone else was who found out. I have never personally told more than a handful of people about it in detail, because I thought it was my burden to carry. I held it in for a long time, feeling ashamed and frustrated that even I couldn't kill myself. It takes an enormous toll on you afterwards. It makes you feel like you are more of a failure in some ways. The depression wore off as soon as I went to rehab after two weeks of being discharged from the hospital. I spent thirty days in a rehabilitation center in North Carolina. I formed a bond there with several other humans I will always keep with me. I was sober for six months after getting out. I relapsed six months later in November of 2009. Nothing went through my mind. I didn't want to harm myself. I wanted to feel human again. It would be another five years before that happened. Today, I am happy and centered. I am spiritual and hopeful. I am the version I had always wanted to be. I promise you it will get better. Live for today. It is worth it. You are worth it. Your cries do not go unheard.

"I once wrote a suicide note, only to wake up and to have been the only one who read it."

When I awoke in the bathtub, I wasn't sure how long I had been passed out for. What seemed like days, turned out to be only 45 minutes or so. I grabbed two bath towels, wrapped them around my arms, stumbled to my bed, still drunk and confused from the pills and tequila. I somehow was able to sleep. I woke up at 3:30am and my roommates were getting ready to go to the base. Before I unwrapped the towels, I asked them not to be mad at me. They looked at me with horror. I will never forget their faces. They rushed me to base. Doc was already there and tended to me before the ambulance showed up. That singular moment was the most embarrassing moment and the lowest point of my life up until then. Everyone was looking at me, as I was being wheeled out on the gurney, wondering what happened. As they got me into the hospital, every single eye was on me. I felt like an alien who was not wanted there. After that, everything is fuzzy, because I eventually blacked out. They couldn't stitch up my arms, because they told me the wounds were too old at the time. They simply wrapped them in gauze and that's how they were kept for the next three weeks. I was in ICU for almost 2 days. About a week later, I went back to the house and found my room untouched. The red ring around the bathtub was still there. I cleaned it all up the best I could. I found my suicide note on my bed the exact way I left it. I read it and then ripped it up. No one else knows what it said, and no one ever will. My story isn't more important than anyone else's, but if we do not talk about mental illness and suicide, more people will die because they will feel as if they can't talk about it. Please know you are not alone. You never will be, it is okay to bring it up. It is okay to share your pain.

Day 1 of 365

My first day of the new year was spent sick in my recliner, watching college football. Not the worst way to spend it. I am so thankful to be where I am at and to be doing what I am doing. I at times forget the struggle and fight it took to be here. Being sick the last few weeks has allowed me to step back and reflect on my year some. It has allowed me to slow down after going non-stop for about nine months. We all need time to sit with ourselves and talk about what hurts, what's missing, what we need, and where to go to next. I am feeling better and will hopefully get back to one hundred percent in a few days, but I don't mind recovering after a year's worth of grinding, growing, and making new realities come true. Never forget to appreciate the ache you had for something once you finally figure it out. It is such a great teacher for the months and years ahead of your life when you find struggle to be more of a friend than an adversary. You don't always have to be your best self. You just need to do your best with the situation you are in and find ways to improve from within.

Injury

For the first time in over two months, I have felt happiness again. I moved out of my old apartment last week and finally healing from a hip bursitis that lasted a month. The sciatic nerve was being pinched as well, so I was as miserable as anyone can be when their body fails them unexpectedly. I am myself again. It has been a difficult stretch for me the past several months, but I never felt sorry for myself or for the situation I was in. I am still where I wanted to be last year. I am still living a life I had dreamt about for ten years leading up to now. The people and things around me have changed, so I am changing, too. Learning to accept that not everything is meant to be forever is a lesson I have been trying to learn since I was a kid, and my parents went through their debacle of a marriage. I still thought if you tried hard enough, things you love and loved could last. Maybe they still do, but I am adapting the best I can, and it will only get better from this point forward. Once you change your mindset and attitude, shit gets extraordinarily better. Once you figure out who you are and what you want, it all makes sense as to why change is necessary and should be a welcomed knock on the door.

Monsters

You will always be too much for some humans. You are not here to seek validation from others. You aren't here to beg for love. You aren't here to sit and waste your time worrying if maybe they are thinking of you as much as you do of them. You aren't here to dwell on the bullshit so many of us get caught up in during our days. Be better than that. Ask more from yourself and make damn sure you are putting and focusing all your energy on things that fucking matter. Make sure you aren't allocating time on some idea of what could have happen if you do this or that. Do something you love and find gratitude for doing it because it's what you wanted to do. Exceed your own expectations. Be your own reason to try more and give up less on your goals. No one is going to hold your hand while you walk to your next destination. Life doesn't work that way once you get older. I didn't even have anyone back then to hold my hand. I walked where I wanted to and it wasn't always the right side of the street, but I still found a way to make it a part of my life and find truth in all my decisions. I can be a horrible friend. I can be a calloused human. I can be the worst person you ever wanted to meet if you push me to the point of making me uncomfortable with your energy. Once I am there, all feelings and intentions go out the window. Savagery at its finest. I'm not proud of it. I am learning how not to be so cold, but there are monsters running around everywhere and it is so easy to be one at times. It isn't difficult for those who had to turn themselves into one because it was the only option left. It seems to be the only time others get the hint to not bring their negative energy and bullshit to my life. Humans will always run back to what's normal, what makes them feel safe, even if it is destined to fail, even if who they love did something incredibly unforgivable to them. It's who some people are. I'm looking for survivors. For the ones who never stop running to the next thing. For the ones who just want to be happy and be forgotten by those who find safety in a comfort zone that withholds all the potential existing within your soul.

Small Victories

For the first time in over five years, I feel sincere happiness. Not just the run of the mill happy, but an elation meant to be experienced by those who have fought off every fucking devil they have ever encountered and every demon they have had to become. I moved out of my old apartment last week and finally beginning to heal from a pinched sciatic nerve I have been dealing with for over a month. It has been the most difficult stretch of living I have had to endure in years, but I never once felt sorry for myself or my situation. I am still where I wanted to be ten years ago. I am still living a life I had dreamt of since I was a kid. The people and things around me have changed, but I am changing, too. I am learning to accept how not everything is meant to be forever. I still thought if you tried hard enough, things you love and loved, could last. Maybe they still do. I am adapting the best I can, and it will only get better from this point forward. Once you change your mindset and attitude, life gets extraordinarily better. Once you figure out who you are and what you want, it all makes sense as to why is necessary and the only constant we get while living.

Queen Size

Before I moved back to Texas, I stopped sleeping in my bed the last few months I was living in Utah. I'm not sure if it was depression or if sleeping on the futon felt more comfortable than sleeping in a queen-sized bed. There was too much of my soul in other areas that when I laid down on the futon, I felt a different comfort, a different peace. Last year took so much of who I was and almost took me beyond the threshold of my own existence in the worst of ways. My anxiety was a s bad as it had ever been. I wasn't happy when I was home. There is something to be said about comfort and what we think of it to be. There is a strong parallel between what we give to others and what is returned to us. I ultimately found common ground to walk on. I gave away every piece of furniture I had bought. There was so much money not necessarily wasted, but given without thought of the future and where I might end up instead of thinking I had it all planned out. My last week there was spent sleeping on the floor. It reminded me of those cold and emboldened nights in Afghanistan, sleeping in the dirt with nothing more than a sleeping bag to protect you from whatever was around you. My simplicity is derived from the childhood I had. If I was comfortable being me, I was happy. I guess my happiness last year was predicated on something I thought I had, but lost years ago now that I think about it. To be back where I couldn't wait to leave, is such a punch in the soul. But my road has never been paved. I have always found solace in the dirt and giving my energy to make sure it is worth the comfort I can give myself. I spent too many years waiting on someone else to find it for me. I am sorry I put that on you. Today, my comfort still breathes in and out when I extend my hand to mother earth, and she gives me a moon to hold and see. Today, it is just a different moon, with a different face and phase on the other side where no one else can see.

Drive-In

I've always loved going to the theater. I wish they had a drive-in here. There is nothing like taking the night off for a few hours and enjoying a movie that can put away your worries and gives you a timeout in life for a little bit. It is like having your ear buds in and listening to some music, while getting lost in the characters you see yourself in or hearing something that slaps some sense into your soul. I do not enjoy hanging out in crowded areas, but a random Wednesday night makes for the perfect night away from the outside world. There is something about being with a few friends or by yourself at the movies that allows you a sense of safety. Once the lights dim and the screen comes alive, the world you live in, disappears long enough to give you a belief of enchantment. Once it is over, you slowly get up, and get back to living.

Top Gun

"What do you want to be when you get older?" I remember them saying it at least every other day. I never knew what I wanted to be when I was younger. I remember the thought of flying planes after I saw Top Gun for the first time. I remember I wanted to be a firefighter after watching Backdraft. I think there are common answers to that question, and I was never a common kid. People always told me that I needed to know so I could pursue something and make life more meaningful. But does it really mean more if you do know? All I wanted to do was matter. I wanted to live and mean something to someone who cared for me, and in return, give them a type of love they never knew they could hold in their heart forever. I had a few rich friends growing up who were wealthy, and still are. They never have to worry about the next day. But I have also met countless humans on bustling street corners who are living with a smile and a warm soul no matter what is going on around them. I am not trying to end up homeless. That isn't the point to all of this. It is just absurd to me that a kid is supposed to have his entire fucking life planned out by the time he gets to be a certain age. Millionaires are half dropouts. Billionaires are a quarter of dropouts. Not everyone is destined for college, or a suit and tie, crunching numbers for other rich people to get even more riche. Happiness is something we are all born with. It is up to us to grow it and spread it from the corners of the world to the outer edges of the universe. Do not become common. Common fucking kills, just as being stuck in routines do. Stretch your mind around new ideas and fucking live, kid. Smile at strangers. Laugh with family and friends as often as you can. Do not force happiness into someone else's life or in your own. It must be natural or else it will die off with the rest of the fake bullshit this world spits out and calls, happy. Learn how to live a life where waking up and getting out of bed means something to you. Strive to be different. This world has all the normal it already needs. There is nothing more to add to its dullness.

Post Office Chivalry

This morning at the post office, I saw an older woman, probably in her late 60's. She was carrying a package and I was about twenty feet or so from the door. I ran to it and opened it for her. I try and do it every time I see someone coming in or going out. She said, "Thank you," and walked in. We were both sending out packages and as soon as I got in line with her, she said, "I didn't know that existed anymore. You don't see that in California at all. It's refreshing that men still hold open the door for women. You surprised me. Maybe chivalry isn't completely dead after all." By the time she got through speaking, my face was blushing a shade of red it isn't accustomed to. There were ten other people in there, all looking at me. I don't handle compliments very well. In fact, it's awkward for me, because I don't see that I am doing anything special or have done anything extraordinary that someone else wouldn't have done. As she was walking out, a thank you came from her again. I smiled and said, "You are welcome." You never know how much of an impact you will have on someone's life if you always do the minimum required. Maybe for some people that's how they live their life, but thankfully, I was raised to always respect and be courteous to everyone around me. We are all fighting something in our lives, and it helps when you can do something as simple as opening a door that will change someone's day for the better.

A Grandmother's Love

When I get to see my family, it is always a great joy for me. Especially during the holiday season when you know everyone will be there and not a lot of words are needed to be said in order to know how much love is in the room. Another year has gone by, and it is funny how much you start thinking about the mornings you woke up and smelled breakfast or heard the silence of a full house as a kid. I have these memories and each time I go through the door, it all comes back to me, as if my grandfather was still alive and waiting on us to finish dinner so we could open presents. Time takes away much of who we are and never gives back what it steals. For the duration of my visit here on earth and wherever my feet decide to jump to next, I will always remember the love a grandmother has for her grandchildren and how she makes them feel all the things they once forgot were real by simply showing you by doing everything in their power to make the house feel not so empty when others couldn't make it. Cherish your families and the time you spend with them. When you hear someone in the kitchen making you something to eat, don't forget to say, thank you. Never forget the woman behind the scenes who'd rather make sure you are taken care of first before she ever grabs a plate for herself.

Eating Alone

I was having lunch today and took a picture of a couple across the table from where I was sitting. I love finding different angles and unique things to view through the camera on my phone. There were three people to the right of their table. An older couple and their son. The mother was having a glass of wine. The father had a Miller Lite longneck. The son had a glass of tea. They talked about expensive needs and items I've never heard of. The wife wanted to fly to Cabo. The father wanted a new vehicle. The son kept drinking his tea. He was probably in his 20s if I had to guess and drove a ford raptor. I'm sure he had all he needed and wasn't too invested in the conversation going on between his mother and father. My attention was directed to an older woman behind them. She was more than likely late 60s and wore Skechers on her feet and a jean skirt, with a turquoise shirt. Her hair was as white as the salt she kept adding to her bread. I was in a booth, and they were all sitting at tables with four chairs. She ordered tea with Splenda and ate the free loaf of bread that she insisted needed more salt. I thought she was waiting on others, but she kept swiping her iPhone to the left and reading news events. How crazy is it, that we are all so similar even when it comes to eating alone. Nothing and no one mattered to her except the phone, bread, and her ability to block out everything else happening around her.

My Pause

Take these wings and help them fly. I've been grounded too long without love, without flight. My heart erupts at the thought of you. There's still life to live while I wait for you, but my pause reflects how much I need you. Love remains the quiet moments when you catch her reading a book and you wish you were the pages being touched and turned. There is nothing greater than finding it in all the things you do for each other. This love I have for you will not be wasted. I can only hope to roam with the flowers of your soul and learn the language of their softness. May love always be the reason. These words I have for you never sleep alongside me. They stay awake in hopes of finding you again.

Where Love Chokes the Death Out of Us All

Rummaging through these old bones of mine, I try and find growth. A sense of maturity that had once escaped me before, now embodies the very human I am. Are we all destined for greatness? Do we have what it takes to continue in order to make our feet move forward? These days are met with mirrors looking back at me with a certain smile I haven't seen in over six years. Am I proud of the man I've become? I will tell you when I finally get to where I belong. A spot reserved for me in the white sands. The feeling of ocean waves cleansing my sins. This is where I shall write and live. You can find me by the majestic shorelines in the years to come. Breathing in life and growing in our love. Once I have found its meaning, with my feet in the waters that once kept me safe, I will make the trek to the mountains to find more of who I need to be. I will gallop around the national parks, using their energies to bend my soul into the contours of pages, full of words and emotions I have needed to release. I will live there in the foothills, at the valley's edge, right where the sun begs the moon to love him forever. Right where love chokes the death out of us all.

Desolation of self and soul

I've been rearranging paintings hanging on the walls of my soul. Yours fit perfectly; a delicate balance of loss mixed with optimistic foreshadowing of where my life seems to be heading. What dreams come to us, depends on what we bring to them. We must be open enough to welcome in the change, the scenery, the panoramic views of loneliness and solitude. My appetite for life never changes. I always end up biting off more than I can chew, more than I can physically digest, but the cost of living isn't cheap. It demands giving all you have and giving up what no longer serves you. It takes humility, a strong structural integrity for things of love. I've been leaning too heavily on my emotions, but they've been the only thing that's kept me standing as of late. I rely on them to configure sentences, pauses, and moments where I say everything no one is ever ready to hear. I don't mind the naked nature of removing who you are to fully evaluate what's happening around you. To see clearly, you must first hear yourself through the white noise we are bombarded with daily. I'm still skimming through old stages of life I've experienced to find what's needed next of me without being asked to search deeper. I live in the abyss, in the desolation of self and soul. I stay on the precipice of love and all its angels. I remain heavily involved in the fight to keep myself from anyone not willing to fight for me. I'm here for the artists who turn whatever demons they have into art, into something beyond the possibility of ever dying. I love the way they bleed like me. I love the way they suffer like me. It's one thing to go through life meeting those who appreciate and see you. It's another thing when you see yourself in their own work, hoping they can do the same with yours. With the gifts we all have, it is imperative to use up every last ounce of them in a pursuit to change the world, to change a life if we are lucky. I cry at the thought of someone out there feeling alone, feeling isolated based on what they are internally harboring without ever being able to release it. Your scars are mine, too.

The Artist

May the devil never know your name. May it be kept away from all that's precious about you and sentenced to the flames. I learned a long time ago how love feels when it comes from a darker place. One where you know it's there, but all you see is red. Some days I wondered if life would ever make sense to me. I wondered how often kids at my age went through hell without ever catching a name. I knew being different was an advantage. I knew being bold with my emotions would eventually get me further away from everything not meant for me. I'm a child of a universe that's constantly changing. I once followed love to the edge of it all, only for it to step away as soon as I asked for a little more. I'm timid at times. I'm a shy, introverted human who is unwilling to waste energy on small talk or try to put together your rhymes. I'm a musician made from beaten down instruments that lost their way, their ability to produce anything but out-of-key notes. I'm made from scraps left by wolves before me, attempting to lure me in close enough to kill me. But they never knew I was born into a darkness, a deep rage of infinite fight. They misunderstood my eyes. They misunderstood their own power when they tried to match mine. I'll turn green before the sun can touch me, before a calming word reaches insider my heart to calm me. Now I walk alone along these paths I've given light to. My enlightening moment came when I was below the rocks, pulled deeper than any human has ever known. I was a wreckage no one wanted to explore. My gold was worthless. My treasure covered in my own blood. All it did was keep away anyone looking for love. It's funny to me how long we voluntarily suffer just for the sake of being miserable. When I came across you, I knew you were something more than an artist. Something more than a mother and goddess. You speak fluently in my sarcasm, my dark and unsettling humor. I see it in the colors you use to be seen by those hopeless enough to think they'll never see daylight again. You broke the sky in-half to find yourself. You paint because it saved you. I see forgiveness all over your hands.

Soul versus Shadow

Every girl I've had a relationship with, is now married or engaged. I think some of us are born to show others the love they deserve, and the rest teach us what self-love is. I'm not sure which one I fall under, but it used to beat me down severely, watching someone you once loved, find love in someone else. I'm not jaded or naïve. I know more times than not, whatever you feel for someone, won't be reciprocated day in and day out. Relationships come and go. They arrive when we need them, when we need a lesson or a new grave to fill. I'm thankful for those who accepted me as I was, all madness, all body made from stone. My life doesn't revolve around what's missing. It breathes for better days. It laughs for jokes untold. I've been extremely critical of myself in the past and even to this day. I've felt as though I gave up too soon, right before the sun kisses the moon. I'm wondering where your colors come from. I wonder how they feel cascading down this sky and into eyes that have been colorblind to certain sunsets based on what someone once said they meant to them. I harness a certain energy, darkened and ripened to the core with decaying angels. It comes from sleepless nights lying awake to hear all my wolves cry. To know they remain hungry after all these years of chasing their prey. It's been a relentless and ongoing task of soul versus shadow. May you never know the old me. The one who killed off anything trying to help me grow. The one who took an axe to his own roots. The one who gave up drugs, but almost didn't give up drinking. I love how you see me. How you never missed a place where my scars made up a story for you to read. You took me in and cared for me like a lover who was hell-bent on saving one more of their own. Someone who almost bled out just to feel something else. You're loved beyond reason, beyond these arms wrapped around you, squeezing all they have left to give. I'm at the end of a rope I tied long ago around my neck, hoping my feet would fail me. Now, it's being used to save what's left of a man climbing out of the devil's hand. I don't need you to save me. I just need you next to me, as I write for you, and you paint for us.

A Precious Sigh

If there's hope for the broken, it all lives and dies with you. I see the way you can love. I see the way you can turn your pain into art. Both captivate me and levitate these feelings even beyond an understanding of my own capabilities. Remain brave for the life you want, for the love you crave, and the feeling of never being full of the awaiting adventure. You're a wonderwall of wondrous graffiti, patiently held together by a sense of wander and prestigious playfulness. You've never existed between the lines of reality, which is why you've always been misunderstood. You're out there beyond heaven and hell. You're a significant source of truth and a beautiful tale of dictating a powerful belief within yourself. Not many can become what you've transformed into. A bed of roses can hold even the most fragile of human frames. It's where you once laid, where you once had to keep yourself safe. You're an opulence of gold and riches. All existing inside your soul. Beauty speaks to those who have yet to see it for themselves, but you've been glowing ever since you were old enough to hold the thorns. You've been struggling to see how defiance can mix with who you are. You tend to make sense out of things that have no meaningful purpose for others. It's why you always get the second glance. It's why you always remain profoundly involved in your own healing. Humans have never been good at keeping love safe. Some have never attended their own funeral before. It's what separates the living from those who are playing by the rules. I look at you and see an unequivocal display of defined chaos working together with a universe that's still trying to catch up to its greatest example of lightning infused with bone. You're a once in a generation kind of feeling. Someone who gets what they want, not for how they look, but for how they work behind the scenes when everyone else has already left. Leading every step of the way, your feet rarely touch the ground others are buried in. You're almost too graceful for this place. I often wonder how far you've traveled to find someone who can keep your attention long enough without you looking away. A precious sigh, you are.

An Abiding Revival

Not many who know me, know how long I've lived outside my structural integrity; the epitome of being homeless within yourself. I've always been leveled by the amount of universal fate that's accompanied me along my journey. It brought me to you, and now, my entirety is back in this restless body of mine. You've given me a new reason to breathe, to take in what's around these trees I'm surrounded by, hoping the storms pass before they kill me. I'm going to need you more than you know. I told you that and you laughed like a child who already knew what love was. I replied with a singular sentence as to why and how I felt that to be how you and I will become one, "because you already know it to be true." Some aspects of life are easily figured out once you've been cast out of your own story multiple times by the same artist who put you into it. I'm beginning to lean against the wind a bit more these days. I've learned from the birds how to migrate to lands meant for me, meant for my keeping. Each winged miracle I watch rise and fall from the sky, provides me an even deeper purpose to give everything a more pronounced and polished try. I stopped looking for love years ago, when it began looking at someone else. I don't resent it. I simply got eaten alive by my own appetite without being fed correctly. I whisper to myself, loud enough so I can hear, but still a quiet hush to not draw attention to who you are. It isn't a prayer I speak, but a note of gratitude I don't have to sing out loud. Thank you for breaking me in-half, into a million fucking pieces so I could learn from my scattering how to find value in what others never cared to put back together properly. A gracious plea for a tenderly made place to rest is what I'm in need of. A spot in the heart of someone who knows how it feels to have the most important thing inside you broken, but still loves anyway, because it's the fucking way of life for so many. My eyes ache from a darkness only I can see. My body trembles at the thought of anyone being close to me who isn't you. I've been alone with my own issues for so long, I've forgotten how it feels to speak about them. You've brought me back to morning, an abiding revival.

Where Everything is Broken

Lay down your armor for me and I'll put away the sword. The fire from the dragon is haunting these bones of mine. I once forgot how to write about things I loved, until you came along and reminded me how they never leave you. I wanted to hold you better, tell you more about my life. A time when everything felt lighter, and I had a more pronounced tone to my voice. Days pass before me, laid to rest softly in their graves. The ones I visit, knowing I didn't give all I had. I think about those out there, all suffering in their own ways. Some of them yell and scream for help. While others open a bottle for their aches. I'm full of every emotion one can emote. Full of every heartbreak a heart can store away. I think about my anger, the limits I've been pushed to. There's a memory I'm hoping for, working towards, and giving my all to. To have open roads before me, no particular destination in mind. Traveling to rid myself of all the baggage I've accumulated along the way. I probably write too much about a love I don't have. I probably stay too close to those who don't love me the same. My sickness is someone else's cure. I once thought forever was a woman, but now I know it's the moon staying up with me until I'm okay. Somewhere out there is the best version of myself, of my potential. I've been making far too many excuses for anyone to know my truth. As the summer gets closer to ending, I can feel fall's outstretched arms readying themselves for me. I've started over so many times, it's been impossible to find my footing, the correct approach to a new beginning. I once thought that was a woman, but now I know it's making better decisions and giving yourself more appreciation for how far one can go when they grab the sun to use in dark moments when nothing else feels right. I miss the connection you feel when words fall short of the moment. I miss the twilight hours when silence sits with you and shares its thoughts about life. I'm going to find a way to get to where I'm going. If I lose people along the way, it's the price we pay in order to arrive promptly to a place not everyone can go. A wanderer never forgets how to fly, how to roam, how to find beauty where everything is broken.

Same name, Different face

Love still seeps from these wounds you gave me. Feelings replace memories on days like these. Where to go to next is the question I'm asking today. Sometimes it feels as though I've captured the castle and now have a wanderer's throne. Pieces of you still litter the streets as musicals play on Broadway tonight. My life will never be the same. I'd like to imagine it for the better, even if I'm still bitter about the way you exited the places we built together. Faces I see, still have your name and each one can only say goodbye to me. Lovers weren't made to be forgotten. Lovers weren't made to be left out in the rain without sunshine breaching through to greet those who suffered the longest with an unbearable pain. The moon still smiles at me, so I guess not all is lost. Even the darkest of nights have her softly made shine. Resting beneath her never will feel the same. Looking out into her fields above the wishes we made become an inviting tale of our souls being saved. I knew the ending was never going to be a victory. I knew the ending was going to keep me on my knees, waving to the mercy you never gave back to me. Lifetimes stretch out before these hands. Emptied out cups that once held a cheers, now only feels like the saddest line ever written. We once loved each other. We once thought it was all that we needed. We once thought love was an equally made set of reasons to suffer a bit longer so we would be able to withstand the loss we had felt all those years ago. I'll never get over this, but I will get over you someday. Right now, I'm trying not to ruin anyone else who wants to be close to me, because I still smell of you. Lessons have always been humans. Lessons have always been excuses we carried alongside our truths, hoping we'd never have to utter the word, defeat. We were something more than love. We were a parallel promise, parceled together by bones and flesh. A kiss pressed out and smoothed over by hands that never wanted to hurt the other. I write from a different place now. I write about a different face now. I write for the empty space next to my heart where yours once rested and slept.

Questionnaire

Each day I get better at knowing who I am. It's been quite a journey to undertake the last several years. Since I was a kid, I always struggled with the idea that we'll know who we are, when we barely know what it is we're after at such a young age. My drinking led me down some hellish roads and paths I didn't know one could take and come back from to speak about. I've met several who have lived a life similar to mine. I know it wasn't as bad as others have had it, but we all have our scars and journals others will never read or see. I learned a long time ago I couldn't live my life without being vulnerable in some sort of way. It was unhealthy for me not to talk about my experiences, my lessons, the dark days that followed me around until I was old enough to correct the pattern. Today, the sun shines on me and I feel its soft and healing nature. I feel the same way about the moon, even if we had a falling out of sorts several years ago now. Both are the lifeblood of who I am. Both feed the animals I keep hidden from view, so no one gets mauled or attacked for not knowing any better. I think everyone does their best with what they were raised on and who raised them. I think we all have our own ideology for the process of finding oneself. The definition and defined nature of it, becomes the foundation of which we build not only friendships on, but relationships. I'm not sure I'll ever be ready for love again, much less throwing myself out there for someone to pick apart, when I'm already severed at the neck. I'm tired of the questionnaire we fill out, asking all the details about who we are, what we do for a living, do we want kids, do you see yourself wanting this or that. It's torturing, especially when you become a certain age. I guess I'm too old to talk about myself or I'm just not that kind of human anymore. Don't get me wrong, I care about finding love and getting to know someone. I'm just taking my time on these roads of mine, experiencing turning left and right or continuing down it until I find a solid shoulder to pull off and rest on for a little while. It hurts being human, but in some ways, everything else hurts if you're not. At least for me that seems to be the truth.

Left Behind

There will come a day when I won't think about you or regret not having done more to save myself from this indelible ache I feel from your absence. But today, it's as fresh as eyes that first found the sun. Certain humans leave different marks on your journey, an unmistakable act of unintentional violence only meant to strengthen your soul. Some come to us as lessons. Others come to us as family, as a preservation of consciousness to save us from following the mistake left behind from those who we once followed. I'm incapable of justifying how I feel without resentment staining every word tossed from the depths of my existence. I worry I won't ever make it out alive. I worry I won't ever make it back up to my feet to try and save my life from the defeat I feel laying beneath life's infinite weight of failure. I've done a lot of wrong during my time on this earth. From locking myself in a bathroom of a friend's house and doing half an eight ball of cocaine with no one else home, trying to keep the demons from getting out. From driving drunk more times than I can remember and only getting pulled over and arrested twice. My age is of no significance to how I feel. I'm still a child at times, looking for his mother to console the crying coming out of every room in the house he ever felt alone in. I was raised by an emotional explosion of anger and angst. I was loved by those same delicate emotions when my misery took ahold of me. I'll never find love again. Half of me believes that. The other half never wants to look for it again. I'm tired from my lack of control for beautiful endings before anything ever begins. In my mind, love is as easily found as it is lost. I still remember writing my suicide note on the night I tried to end it all. The song I had playing in my room on repeat. The temperature of the bath water as I got in, naked and welcoming whatever came next. I don't dwell on my past to feel sorry for myself. I think of it fondly as a tool for my growth, maturity, and perspective, when I feel as though I have nothing left to give. I'm optimistic about everything, because I believe in purpose, in the end of the world only being a goodbye said too soon, too early, way before the night shimmers in your madness. I'm nothing more than being someone who was told they were loved, only to find out those who give all, end up losing even more in the end.

The Hello That Changed My Life

We loved in a life that has since passed us both by. What we were will never be again. What we had will never be given again. Growing up, I was unaware of how many times a heart could die, but still have the strength to keep going, to keep existing in a body that refused to believe in goodbyes. Love is nothing more than a delicacy that can starve you if you let it. I have known all kinds of humans while I've been on earth. The good ones, the shy ones, the ones you don't know you need until you are at the very bottom of a page you read a million times but never understood its reason for ending the way it did. I've grown accustomed to the customary remarks handed out by those with hate in their eyes and jealousy seeded deeply within their seething for a better life. Many of us will never get another chance to chase after the fire once it goes out. Many of us will be on bended knee, ultimately believing promises are a way out. I was meant to find you and I did so without hesitation, even when I knew I was going to lose you to someone else. I never once tried to change your mind, because when it comes to love, the heart is where it all begins and ends. It's been quite a journey for me to get to this point, to this defined resolution of my own evolution. A sturdy soliloquy made from interior proclamations set forth the chain of events I'm still holding firmly. I thought all things destined to be found, would come without a cost, without a loss of life chalked out in some unforeseen scene. I would've given anything to have assured your safety from your fears. Not even all the gods and angels could keep hell from reaching where I was to keep me down. At the end of the day, I'm chasing a flame that won't burn out. In some ways, I'm grateful for your presence which keeps me from falling down beyond the seventh circle. We all grow tired of being who we are. It's why we lose ourselves to characters we read about, to the drinks that keep us from interfering in reality and living in a moment we're unsure exists. It's why we end up becoming penniless, unable to afford anything more than a smile that tells someone, we're okay. Your hello changed the course of my life.

The Fisherman

Most nights I hide behind the lie that you still love me. That if things were different, we'd still be together. I'm not sure if I digest life properly or if there's an easier way to eat broken glass to kill what's hurting inside. I'm not dramatic. I'm honest. I'm not chaotic. I'm a stretched-out version of normal. I know if the sun would die tomorrow and leave fresh embers on the ground, I'd do all I could to keep you warm until winter was over. I fell in love today with a dancing shadow of leaves upon a brick home. It reminded me of how precious everything is and what kind of mark we leave on things even after we're gone. The branches were abandoned a few weeks ago, but in my mind, I could still see what was once there. That's how I feel you. That's how I see you today. I'm tortured by a childhood I never had. I'm split in-half by a life I've been keeping together by a set of docile hands, clenched around parts of me that don't want to be together. My heart is somewhere in-between a stutter and a goodbye. It skips along the pavement with me as if it's a pet I picked up to keep me company, instead of keeping me alive. I wish love were easier on the mind. I wish it were a simplified version of what I once thought it could be as a child. But I'm not sure I ever knew it to be anything other than someone leaving. Some days it's bearable, knowing you gave your all to a personified embodiment of all things living, of all things desperate to survive a war you never started, but grabbed a weapon anyway. Light sharpens light, just as darkness evokes an unfamiliar foe. I'm learning more about what I'm after, instead of what I no longer have. Some things are less complicated once you begin to organize a closet full of random skeletons you can finally hang up and put a name to. This life of mine dangles hope in front of me, as if I'm a fisherman with nothing attached to my own hook. It's a symbolic approach to knowing what you don't need in order to succeed and have a full belly from the dreams just big enough to fit inside your net. I've walked in waters above my knees long enough to know the further you go out alone, the deeper the hurt is.

Murphy's Law

I spent so long wondering if I was good enough for you, I forgot if I was actually good enough for myself. When you give all you have to someone, you forget how empty it feels not having anything left when they leave, because they'll always leave. I wish I could paint you a better picture of life, of love, of a predestined miracle. I wish I had more descriptive words for how it feels to be completely annihilated by someone you never thought could do you a single ounce of harm. All I have left to use are black and white photos to conserve whatever energy remains inside of me. I'm tired of being positive all the time, when I know more than likely, the devil gets his laugh from those who think that way. I'm optimistic at heart, an aesthetically pleasing sentence of life and death, decorated with black roses and skulls from those who had nothing else to give me. Not all is lost when you lose everything. A scattering occurs, a velvet display of song and shine. You look everywhere to find something to keep you upright and focused on the next journey, on the next endeavor set out beyond your bones and parcels of earth. I wondered for a long time if I was the singular problem, the unenforceable inhabitant of Murphy's Law. I still wonder if I'm the root of all evil or simply an exposed and damaged nerve in a gathering of humanity. I wish I could tell you it gets better, but some of us are chosen to be born for a suffering many will never experience, so others can learn about it through writing, through someone's absence. I believe we are all connected in some way or another. Maybe by the ended of the year, happiness will collide against my face and break away the sadness attached to these eyes, this smile, to every fucking part of my existence. My position has yet to change about love. I may have slid over a little more, away from someone else's definition of it, but like the moon, it finds you regardless of light or emptied out sky. We're all after something. I'm fortunate this is my journey and no one else's. I've been suffering since I was a child. If I must continue to do so in order to realign myself with this path, I will. I'm a proponent for change, for a swift reckoning of diluted truth.

A Day in My Noose

I've heard people say, "spend some time in my shoes, walk around and get comfortable with being uncomfortable." I guess my shoes are tired, too. If you want to get to know me, spend a day in my noose, the wrapping around of all my inconceivable thoughts about life and love. Maybe then you'd be able to feel a tightening you're actually comfortable with. It isn't all black and white, though some would argue until they're blue in the face. There's an infinite amount of feelings to be talked about, yet we struggle to explain ourselves to friends and family. Being a middle child, I was a sounding board before I knew how to console my own pain and give it space in a life where grief became the foundation for my solitude. I'm not a scary person. I've never hurt anyone who didn't deserve it. The bravest thing I ever did was comfort those who were hurting, all the while, braving my own suffering for the sake of making sure someone else didn't feel alone. Maybe good enough is all some of us get. Maybe that's all there is for misfits and deranged lunatics who never fit into a society constantly blaming everyone else but themselves. I feel lucky to be me. Though if I'm being honest, there were a few times in my life where I was driving by myself and wanted to jerk the wheel all the way to the left. Those thoughts aren't normal I don't believe, but they helped me see through my own misfortunes growing up. I've been a helper ever since I learned how to hold my hands up to keep the sun from going down. I've never been scared to be on my own, but to be without love, well, that's the beauty and sacrifice of being a human. We're all running rampant in our own lives. Hurrying past the endearing hugs and unfathomable goodbyes. There's a race some of us are running. I'm just hoping to slow down for a few years to understand the path I'm on and if I'm doing enough to manifest a future. I'm going to create a life so goddamn unbreakable, when someone asks me if I'm happy, I'll point to the light coming out of me. I'm in love with everything these days. For the first time, that includes my own presence within it. The air feels lighter now. The choking has come and gone.

Hope to Hold

You belong somewhere besides looking into a mirror trying to find what others don't love about you. Your beauty isn't easily defined, because it is infinite, a paused reflection of time itself. I need you to see what the moon saw that night, as it laid out the stars for you. I need you to know you're a single wave comprised of years of fight that made you this way, this indelible sensation of a storied victory march. All I have are these stories about you. Someone I once loved. Someone I once held. Someone I'm still mourning in the quiet hours of my morning and late at night when my hands clench due to the lack of strength to let you go. You're everything I wanted loved to be. You're everything I thought the beginning of a life should feel like. You're everything I had hoped to be looking back at me, staring a hole in my goddamn heart, because that's where you knew you wanted to stay. I've been trying to wash away your scent, your marks, your caption-less looks you once gave to me when we found comfort in our togetherness. There are still pieces of you lodged inside of my life, destined to become another tale of what I don't have anymore. For some reason, you have stayed with me all these years, like a monster underneath a bed of a child who checks to make sure it's gone, but knows it never leaves. Some days I feel as though we'll find each other by accident again. Maybe love will always feel like an abandonment to me. I know you're still important to my story, to my life, and for those reasons, I'll never leave you even though you left me to deal with this misery. If you find yourself, years from now, feeling alone and broken, remember that I said to you. Remember what I told you. Your pain is my pain. What happens to you, happens to me. You're everything I never wanted to miss. You're someone I never wanted to know, because I knew it would have to take you leaving for me to finally let you go. It's how we survived the way we did. It's how we thrived becoming who we were. It's why I'll always look down at my hands and remember your fingers still being interlocked with mine. It's always going to be you who I hope to hold.

An Endless Story

One thing about her, is the magic she was born with. Her love for adventure creates an infinite fullness, a righteous feeling of flying. When you're near her, you finally understand the moon and all her stars a little bit better. The purpose means nothing without steady work and sacrifice. When you approach her, you'll feel her wings made from colors shared by many, but never seen by anyone else. They tell a story of where it all began, and where it will always lead those crazy enough to love. I hope you find her. I hope you are able to be close enough to her at least once in this life. It is where I found and learned how to be human. It is where I learned how to properly function without failing who I was.

Graveyard Shift

I want to empower people to travel more, to love themselves more, to worry less about life, and just do your best for the day set forth before you. I want them to see someone like me can have some kind of success, even after all the bullshit I've been through. I want them to chase after what they want and not allow fear to keep them from doing it. I want others to know you don't get anywhere in life if you continue telling yourself, "I'll get there tomorrow." Live your life without any more excuses. If you want to travel, go do it. If you love someone, tell them. If you want more, get yourself where you need to be, mentally, physically, and spiritually. By not doing what we want with where are in life, we are killing any chance of ever having it. I want you to know it's okay not to know a goddamn thing about anything. It shouldn't keep you from learning more about yourself and what you deserve. Stop taking the backseat in your own story. Learn how to drive it, how to steer it, how to navigate it by any means necessary. Find more. Talk less. Actions instead of words, allow us to put everything into perspective. I promise you, if you keep waiting, you are going to miss out on the most spontaneous and brilliant moments of your life. It is such a travesty watching those living, dig their graves each day, without knowing they are soon to be inside them, because they know nothing else but routine, safety, and waiting.

Hello

We want to explore the possibility that something greater is out there. We want to know that we aren't alone in our feelings and emotional states. We want to eat new foods and discover new origins of what makes everyone fall in and out of love. We at times choose to sit in the peace and quiet, with only a few lights on above our heads and look out of windows. We don't want to care about what's going on around us, but when we are still, it is only then we understand how much it makes us who we are. I look out of my window and see a sun bursting with laughter and a palm tree waving at everyone as they go by, never noticing the friendly gesture. It waves to me, and I wave back. I learned a long time ago to be appreciative of all living things. They are here to teach us, and I will not allow a day to go by and not acknowledge what has survived to wish me well and take time to say hello.

Today

Some days I wake up and still cannot believe I made it this far in life. I cannot believe I came back from where I was and where I took myself all those years ago. At times, I want to kiss the fucking ground to show how thankful I am. Misery and chaos have shaped me. I am not normal. I am absent of morals, of common decency when it comes to the easy way of living. I take pride in being different from others. I never set out to be that way. I enjoy getting tattoos. I enjoy not having to drink at all to be happy or escape this life. I enjoy writing when I want to and not because I have to. I've never forced anything in my life, except when it came to love. I've always went with what the universe threw at me and allowed me to. I didn't know it then, but my rock bottom was my mountain. It was my beginning. It was almost the ending, but the cosmos had different plans for me. I am still looking for answers I'll probably never find. I guess that's the joy of my life; knowing I might not find it all before it ends. The journey from place to place, connection to connection, feeling to feeling, I am so grateful I found a place to call my own. I grew up never knowing who would show up or who would leave. Being in a broken home, you're left wondering for years what the hell happened and why. You stumble in at 3am, half drunk and high, hoping you can just sleep for a few days without being interrupted by screaming or fighting. You wish it would all go away until you're ready for it. Some days I wake up and can still feel those years, but they don't bother me like they once did. I made peace with that part of my life years ago. I have a relationship with my mother. I never thought that would've been possible back then. I have a relationship with my father. I'll always call him regardless of time or day, because I know he will answer and hear me out. My younger brother is my best friend. I couldn't be any happier for the life he has made for himself. My older brother has a beautiful family and made something inspiring for others, including myself. I've always been the poster child for rebellion and solitude. I started smoking cigarettes before I was a teenager. Someone who had his first beer before that. Someone who has tattoos and goes there for therapy more than the ink itself. Someone who dropped out of college twice because he never could settle his demons the night before and needed something more than a professor who spoke about things I cared nothing about. I was a child made for war. My narrative changed right before I volunteered for the Marines. I write now to release my pain instead of drowning it. I guess they both kill the feeling, but one keeps them above the ground. I have ten notebooks full of writings I hope to turn into more books in the coming years. It's okay to be fucking happy with loving who you are and doing what you've always wanted to do. Tomorrow is my empty page. Live it all for today.

Before another Breath

This is something we are unfamiliar with, these feelings, these thoughts, these unknown possibilities. I've been wanting to learn you better. The pieces of you kept behind the moon for only you to see, those are the ones I am after. I could tell you all about my life, but if I am being honest, moving forward, I want it to be about you. We will take it slow and see where it all goes. The ocean tells me secrets you've thrown into her waves, hoping they would sink before sunlight could touch them. I cannot wait to see you and finally meet you. To see you in the flesh will be the awakening of my soul. It will be the birth of every idea and sensation I have fathered since I was a child. I want to try for you, for the life you are made of. I want to give you and show you what is capable of happening when effort is matched, and adoration sings to lonely bones breaking under the weight of the world. I want to help you in every fucking way I can. I want to be your best friend and someone you can always run to when the horizon tries swallowing you whole. Over time, you've become my words, and with that, you've become my life's work. I have no idea what the future holds for us, but I will try and give you something beautiful you can hold onto when night comes for your peace. I don't know what I am doing if I'm not trying to get closer to you in some way. You are such a light for me to look at. You are my direction, my truth, and an escape I no longer need to be afraid of, because you are here now. There are still several talks and expressions needed to be uncovered, but I've waited this long for you, and I won't come up for air until I feel your breath touch mine. This year has been hellish, chaotic, and such a loss for many of us. I found your rapture this year amongst my own setbacks. To know you are in my life now like this, I would have to say it's been the most meaningful one yet. You're the chapter where everything else will begin. I'll walk with you on the beach, street, or down the aisle. Whatever it fucking takes to be with you. There's love, then there is something beyond meaning. It is where I find myself with you.

Ghostly

Not all ghosts are the same. Some stick around to inflict more unreasonable pain than is needed. They're the constant reminder of what could've been, of what will never be again. Others tend to your wounds. They show up unannounced, but it's okay, because they know who you are inside and out. You'll be the formidable force that allows my voice to never weaken, that keeps other hauntings away from my peace. It's a strange thing to witness when the moon sinks below your eyes. I can still see your light. You weren't going to be forgotten by me. Whether it ended before it did or somewhere down a path we knew was unsustainable for us. I've written about you for an entire lifetime it seems. My body only knows how to move with yours. My hands only know how to frame out a dream where you are the singular reason behind such things. You're the fire against the blade. A proven source of belief, when all I had before was doubt covering every single part of who I was before you. I lay down at night, turn on my right side, and imagine you there again. We never had a chance to sleep in the same bed, make love in a room of our own. We never had time to figure out what it would be like if we actually made it through the obstacles we were being faced with. We never had more than a few days together, but in that short amount of time, all pain faded, all memories wiped clean of what living once was for me. I spoiled you as much as I could. Be it with words, small gestures of love, or a few gifts I got you while I was on vacation out there. I've never cried before when someone left. I've never felt such a sharpness and emptiness when you decided for me that you would leave. You were the surest thing my body felt when it came to someone else's warmth. I know I still need you, and that's where I don't say anything more. It isn't what you should hear from me. I'm not your person anymore., I wait patiently for a sunset to come. It's when I feel your colors against mine. The vibrancy of love and all its offspring is still you. You shift all universes, and me.

You in Every Way

Here's the truth, I never thought I'd love again after her. You came along and showed me something different, a preciousness without harm. I won't ever be able to think of love and it not be you. You didn't ruin me. You changed my entire perspective of what we can endure, of what we are worthy of having, even if it doesn't stick around for the ending. If it isn't you, all I'll do is ruin anyone who thinks they can love me or wants to be with me. It's tragic, I guess. It's apropos as well. When we found each other, I finally felt something other than my own demons playing with my bones and breaking my dreams over them. It felt as though I was stumbling out of my own darkness and there you were, holding a smile fit for a victory I had never known of. You freed me from completing another disastrous attempt at being human, when I hadn't been one of those in years. I was too reckless for my own good, drinking away what was left of my youth. I'll never completely understand your leaving and why it ended as abruptly as it started, but I know we weren't meant for a lifetime. I take you wherever I go. I can only write about you, because it's always been about you. In this distance between hearts, my body embodies a celestial sensation made from galaxies and moons no longer close enough for me to see. The time twists and bends itself around my mind, making me believe you'll always love me, but I honestly think you'll never stop. Maybe that's the hardest part of all. Maybe knowing I'll never be able to be with anyone else and not see you is the endless curse I'll carry with me until my head falls off. You were worth it then, and you are worth it now. Whatever is inside of me, whatever attached itself to you over the years, it won't let you go. I've tried to leave it where you left it, but even on my thousandth try, it still clings to you, as the sun embraces a moon it will always burn for. Humans come and go in our lives. It's been that way since chaos found us and turned us into whatever this existence is. I can write all I want about it. I can speak until my tongue is bitten off and rolls slowly down my throat. Even then, my soul will find a way to yours.

Scattered, but whole

She's mostly scattered across the sky these days, but still has time for herself when love is what she is need of. When a breath finds her. When an idea brushes up against her heart. When the night beckons her to dance, and she accepts willingly with open arms. When the life she has built needs her to relax, she finds it in calm waters and subtleties gathered throughout the day. Her soul has dreams older than earth itself, which keep her grounded. Her eyes have held more than just a glance at the moon. There is no single right way to love or to care for someone like her. You just hope your best can run wild with hers and be there when all the stars collapse and create a moment when everything is where it's supposed to be. Where life wakes you up gently to ask if you want to see the sunrise, has a cup of coffee in its hands, and walks you out softly. Your feet will never be touching the coldness of what this earth has given you before.

Victory in Light

I needed someone like you, then you showed up. A togetherness may be nothing more than knowing the other exists. If that is how love should be for me, if that is what love is now for my life, I am comforted. I am content with these thoughts of you, this sensation of desire and embrace. My fate has already been written. I'm simply trying to add your name somewhere inside it. You are energy. You are light. You are love in every season. You are adventure. You are grace. You are home to my bones. You are wild. You are ambitious. You are all things precious. You are galaxies. You are present. You are in love with every minute. You are a gentle embrace of chaos fort those who have missed out on their own. You are the eyes opening right before the nightmare kills you. You are freedom. You are above all, everything to me. Stay young in everything you do and all the places you go. A soul never forgets the moon, and she will always remember the woman who gave her back her light.

Guts & Glory

I keep breaking hearts faster than I can put mine back together. I've loved extremely hard my entire life. All too often it brought me another unmarked grave to fill. Someone I once loved is married and expecting a child now. Someone else I once loved, left me to start another life with an old flame. She's engaged now. Love will always cost you a life. You never know if it is the old one or the future one. My heart has ended up hurting others. I am sorry for the way I have broken myself for it all. There is nothing more profound or brave than gutting yourself to see what pours out. I am imagining the sight I will learn upon my insides being cleansed by truth, by hindsight, by the ability to value where I stood up and proclaimed being lost was nothing more than finding another way to you.

www.ingramcontent.com/pod-product-compliance
Lightning Source LLC
Chambersburg PA
CBHW082336300426
44109CB00046B/2506